Persuasive Writing

WRITING 4

AUG 15

SADDLEBACK
EDUCATIONAL PUBLISHING

WRITING 4

Descriptive Writing

Expository Writing

Narrative Writing

Persuasive Writing

SADDLEBACK
EDUCATIONAL PUBLISHING
www.sdlback.com

© 2005, 2011, 2013 by Saddleback Educational Publishing

ISBN-13: 978-1-62250-027-7
ISBN-10: 1-62250-027-X
eBook: 978-1-61247-670-4

Printed in the United States of America

17 16 15 14 13   1 2 3 4 5

Contents

To the Student

How about it? Can you count on your writing skills to make your meaning clear?

Check yourself out by answering the following questions!

▶ Can you give other people easy-to-follow directions and explanations?

    EXAMPLES: **how to tape a TV show**
                      how a bill becomes law

▶ Can you describe something clearly enough to create a vivid image in the minds of your audience?

    EXAMPLES: **a dramatic thunderstorm**
                      a movie star's mansion

▶ Can you tell a story so well that your audience is fascinated from beginning to end?

    EXAMPLES: **the history of baseball**
                      the world's worst date

▶ Can you usually persuade others to accept your opinion or take some kind of action?

    EXAMPLES: **see a certain movie**
                      register to vote

Saddleback's WRITING 4 series will improve your written work—no matter what your purpose is for writing. If you make your best effort, the result will surprise you. You'll discover that putting words on paper isn't that much different from saying words out loud. The thought processes and grammatical structures are the same. Writing is just another form of expression; skill develops with practice!

Competent writers do better at school and at work. Keep that in mind as you work your way through these books. If you learn to write well, you're more likely to succeed in whatever you want to do!

Are you ready to go for it? Follow me—I'm off and running!

Lesson 1

Reasons for Writing

Every piece of writing—from a short note to a long novel—is written for a reason. Perhaps the writer's goal is to tell a story or to describe a person or a place. Or it may be to explain why an event happened, or to urge the reader to take action.

A. Use words from the box to complete the sentences about four kinds of writing with different goals. If any words are unfamiliar, look them up in the dictionary.

expository	narrative	persuasive	descriptive

1. _____ writing attempts to convince the reader that a particular idea has merit.

2. _____ writing tells a story, usually relating events in chronological order.

3. _____ writing creates a picture in the reader's mind of an object, event, or person.

4. _____ writing explains an opinion, process, or idea, often by using a definition or a cause and effect.

B. Write an example sentence to demonstrate each of the four "reasons for writing." Be sure that your purpose is clear.

1. DESCRIPTIVE: _____

   _____

2. NARRATIVE: _____

   _____

3. PERSUASIVE: _____

   _____

4. EXPOSITORY: _____

   _____

The *tone* of your writing reflects your attitude toward the subject. Depending on your purpose, the tone of your composition changes. It might, for example, be *straightforward, sarcastic, outraged,* or *mysterious.* Tone is a major ingredient of style. It sets the mood of your composition.

C. Write **persuasive**, **narrative**, **descriptive**, or **expository** after each item. Then identify tone by writing *straightforward, sarcastic, outraged,* or *mysterious.*

1. The bright orange flames rose higher and higher in the inky midnight sky. The exhausted firefighters were nearly overcome by acrid fumes and intense heat. The shrill wail of shrieking sirens filled the air. The chief was sure it was arson. But who had set the blaze . . . and why?

   TYPE OF WRITING: _____ TONE: _____

2. Take the Greenbelt Freeway north to the second downtown exit. Go right on Market Street until it dead ends at Polk. Then turn left and stay in the left-hand lane for about half a block. Turn left at Valleyview and pull up at the first brick house on the right-hand side of the street. I'll be watching for you.

   TYPE OF WRITING: _____ TONE: _____

3. "Oh, *sure* I believe you," Andrea snarled. "Why *wouldn't* I believe you? Just because you 'forgot' your promise never to use my car without permission? Just because you told everyone the secret you'd sworn never to tell? *Of course* I believe you. *Not.*"

   TYPE OF WRITING: _____ TONE: _____

4. Mayor Pocketstuffer should be prosecuted rather than reelected! Even his own staff members were stunned to discover evidence of his brazen misuse of public funds. Because of him, our once prosperous city is now bankrupt! I urge all concerned citizens to speak out at tonight's town hall meeting.

   TYPE OF WRITING: _____

   TONE: _____

Lesson 2

Writing to Persuade

When you write to *persuade*, your goal is to influence the reader's point of view. Perhaps you want the reader to reconsider an opinion. Or perhaps you're trying to convince the reader to *do* something (vote) or to *stop* doing something (littering).

A. Think about the different purposes of various kinds of writing. Then study the items below and circle only examples of *persuasive* writing.

wedding announcement	lost-and-found ad	movie review
car repair instructions	dialogue for a play	political speech
anti-smoking poster	newspaper editorial	gardening manual
army recruitment brochure	employee handbook	narrative poem

B. Suppose you are assigned to write a weekly editorial column for your school newspaper. What ideas do you want to promote? What issues are most important to you? Express your viewpoint by writing two persuasive sentences about each topic.

1. **school uniforms** _____

_____

_____

_____

2. **teacher's pets** _____

_____

_____

_____

3. **the grading system** _____

_____

_____

_____

4. **the food in the cafeteria** _____

_____

_____

_____

C. *Demand* and *beg* are two quite different verbs that describe persuasive action. There are many others. Think about the verbs in the box. Then number them from 1 to 4 to rank the intensity of persuasion from weakest to strongest.

_____ **threaten**

_____ **plead**

_____ **entice**

_____ **recommend**

Now read the statements below. Then write **T** (threaten), **P** (plead), **E** (entice), or **R** (recommend) to identify the different forms of persuasion.

1. _____ **BIOHAZARDOUS ZONE. Do not enter! Violators will be prosecuted.**

2. _____ **Free hot dogs and soft drinks at our Grand Opening Celebration!**

3. _____ **Simple baking soda is an effective remedy for heartburn.**

4. _____ **My behavior was inexcusable. Please forgive me!**

D. Now write two original sentences as an example of each form of persuasion.

1. **a recommendation** _____

_____

_____

_____

2. **a plea** _____

_____

_____

_____

3. **a threat** _____

_____

_____

_____

4. **an enticement** _____

_____

_____

_____

Lesson 3 Propaganda

Are there any special ways to "sell" an idea or a product? Writers who want to influence others have developed a variety of methods to do just that. Read about six common *propaganda techniques* in the chart below.

NAME CALLING	• Applying a prejudicial label to someone or something in order to discredit it *a pie-in-the-sky proposal*　　　　*a big spender*
GLITTERING GENERALITY	• Using a beloved or highly esteemed word or idea in order to win approval without close examination *the patriotic choice*　　　　*like your mom's cooking*
BANDWAGON	• Urging you to "join the crowd" by doing something that "everyone else" is supposedly doing *Join all your friends and neighbors!*　　*Don't be the last to own one!*
TESTIMONIAL	• Quoting a well-known person in favor of a certain product or policy *"Hollywood stars like me depend on Bald-No-More. You can, too!"*　　*"My teammates and I eat Health-O-Meal before every game!"*
RED HERRING	• Diverting attention from the real issue by focusing on secondary or irrelevant facts *The handsome candidate, a daily jogger, has been married for 24 years.*　　*Our laundry product smells like lemons and comes in a pretty package.*
WITHHOLDING FACTS	• Misleading by leaving out relevant facts that don't support the desired point of view *charged with jury tampering (no mention that the case was dismissed for lack of evidence)*　　*removes rust stains from anything (no mention that it often causes skin to blister)*

Many people associate the word *propaganda* with dishonesty. But in itself, propaganda is neither good nor bad. It all depends on where and for what purpose it is used. Bias or preference is appropriate in a statement of editorial opinion. In a news story, however, only complete, unbiased facts should be reported.

EDITORIAL

Do we want to attract new business to our city? If so, the new city hall is vital. The old building is way too small, and structural experts claim that it's dangerous!

Joe Citizen

NEWS REPORT

Opinion is divided about plans for a new city hall. Some say it's an absolute necessity, while others argue that it's a waste of taxpayers' money.

Joe Journalist

A. Think about the different types and possible uses of propaganda. Then write
T or **F** to tell whether each statement below is *true* or *false*.

1. ____ Language can mold a reader's
thinking to a great extent.

2. ____ Words like *barbarity* and *cruelty*
arouse unfavorable attitudes.

3. ____ Propaganda never encourages
our desire to flatter ourselves.

4. ____ Most people know how to recognize
the tricks of propaganda.

5. ____ Favorable publicity cultivates
the good will of the public.

6. ____ Words like *justice* and *health*
have a positive impact.

B. Now be creative! Write a one- or two-line example of five of the six propaganda
techniques described on page 10.

1. *promotion for an American Red Cross blood drive*

   TECHNIQUE: _____

   EXAMPLE: _____

   _____

2. *ad for a new toothpaste*

   TECHNIQUE: _____

   EXAMPLE: _____

   _____

3. *politician's comments about his opponent*

   TECHNIQUE: _____

   EXAMPLE: _____

   _____

4. *appeal for contributions to aid victims of a disaster*

   TECHNIQUE: _____

   EXAMPLE: _____

   _____

5. *editorial argument for a new city swimming pool*

   TECHNIQUE: _____

   EXAMPLE: _____

   _____

Prewriting: Audience Viewpoint

Before you begin to write, spend some time thinking about your audience. Why? The more you know about your target audience, the more effective your message will be.

Be aware that different audiences have different experiences, beliefs, and opinions. Their viewpoints are often based on different fears, wants, and needs.

A. Here's a chance to show what you already know about differences among audiences. Circle the word that correctly completes each sentence.

1. Ads for (arthritis / acne) medicine are usually targeted to teenagers.

2. Gun control is a primary interest of (police officers / big business owners).

3. (Security / Popularity) is a major concern of senior citizens.

4. (Adults / Teenagers) are more likely to object to loud music.

5. (Merchandisers / Minorities) would probably support a candidate who fights against prejudice.

6. (Army generals / Pacificists) usually believe that nuclear weapons should be banned.

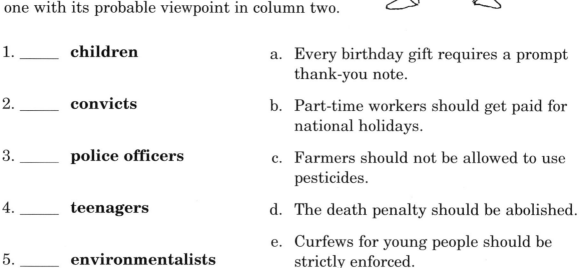

B. Write a letter to match each audience in column one with its probable viewpoint in column two.

1. _____ **children**

2. _____ **convicts**

3. _____ **police officers**

4. _____ **teenagers**

5. _____ **environmentalists**

6. _____ **grandparents**

a. Every birthday gift requires a prompt thank-you note.

b. Part-time workers should get paid for national holidays.

c. Farmers should not be allowed to use pesticides.

d. The death penalty should be abolished.

e. Curfews for young people should be strictly enforced.

f. Cotton candy should be served in the school cafeteria.

Even members of the same group don't *always* agree. In fact, intelligent people often have *very* different ideas about the same topic. Something that strikes one person as outlandish might seem perfectly reasonable to someone else. It all depends on your point of view.

"A good neighbor keeps to himself, minds his own business, and respects the privacy of others." ←→ *"A good neighbor is a close family friend who's always on hand to help in an emergency."*

"Football is a violent, dangerous sport that should be banned from all high school campuses." ←→ *"Football builds school spirit and teaches important life lessons to young student-athletes."*

C. Think about the following object or topic from two or three very different points of view. First, write a sentence or two describing each viewpoint. Then write another sentence explaining the likely *reason* for that viewpoint.

1. TOPIC: *paying teenagers to do household chores*

   TEENAGER: _____

   _____

   REASON: _____

   PARENT: _____

   _____

   REASON: _____

2. OBJECT: *flowering cherry tree in springtime*

   BIRD: _____

   _____

   REASON: _____

   ARTIST: _____

   _____

   REASON: _____

   WOODWORKER: _____

   _____

   REASON: _____

Lesson 4 — Writing Persuasive Topic Sentences

A *topic sentence* expresses the main idea in a paragraph. It gives the reader an immediate idea of what to expect. (It also helps the writer stick to the point!)

When you're writing persuasively, it's especially important to make your first sentence crystal clear. Why? Because an excellent topic sentence will capture the reader's interest. What you *don't* want is for the reader to stop reading before you've "made your pitch"!

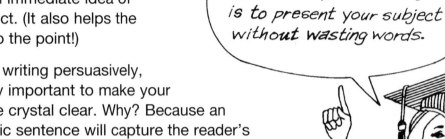

Effective topic sentences get right to the point. Your goal is to present your subject without wasting words.

A. Cross out unnecessary words in the following topic sentences. Then rewrite the sentences on the lines, adding only words that contribute to meaning. The first one has been done as an example.

1. ~~This paragraph is about~~ the benefits of physical exercise.

   Physical exercise has many benefits.

2. We were assigned to write an ad for a new product, so I'm writing about *Acneaway*.

   _____

3. You may not agree with me, but honesty really is the best policy.

   _____

4. Some people think there are too many commercials on TV.

   _____

B. Improve the topic sentences below. Eliminate unnecessary words and add just enough interesting information to introduce your subject.

1. I urge you to vote for Vic Vargas, although I don't know much about him.

   _____

2. Even though its parking lot is inadequate, the museum is a good place to visit.

   _____

3. I'm fairly sure it takes more talent to ski than to ice skate.

   _____

4. The details are pretty boring, but you should know the facts about
   credit card debt.

   _____

5. *The Revenge of the Earthworms* was screened for the first time last night.

   _____

C. Think about the information in the paragraphs below. Then write an interesting,
well-worded topic sentence to begin each paragraph.

1. _____

   As well as being a gifted natural athlete, Hawks quarterback Mike Mack
   is superbly conditioned. He is also a quick thinker who always makes
   good decisions under pressure. By comparison, the Bobcats' quarterback,
   Wally White, needs more training and experience to compensate for his
   average natural abilities. Can he think fast in pressure situations? He
   hasn't proven it yet.

2. _____

   The expensive *FatMelt* earrings advertised on television are like the
   Pounds-Off powdered supplement offered in newspaper ads. They are
   equally effective—which is to say, <u>not</u>. *Inches Gone* "liquid lunch" and
   Slim-New-You "willpower pellets" fall into the same sorry category.
   All claim to reduce fat, but the only thing they actually reduce is the
   amount of money in your wallet!

3. _____

   As your big brother, I'm telling you that you're making a big mistake.
   You can't break your word to Dad and then pretend that it never
   happened! You don't think you have to admit that you're wrong? You
   don't think you have to promise to mend your ways? *In your dreams!*
   If you want Dad to forgive and forget, you'll have to show him some
   common courtesy—and *soon!*

Lesson 5

Persuasive Paragraphs 1

A *paragraph* is defined as a group of sentences about one idea. A good paragraph needs at least three sentences to support the topic sentence. These supporting sentences make up the body of the paragraph.

A variety of details may be used to develop the idea presented in the topic sentence. Supporting details may be facts or examples. They may make comparisons or answer questions raised by the topic sentence.

A. Read the topic sentences. Then circle two letters to identify appropriate supporting details.

1. *Good neighbors take good care of their yards.*

   a. Herbicides do an effective job of killing crabgrass.

   b. It takes only about 15 minutes to mow a small lawn.

   c. Trashy yards lower neighborhood property values.

   d. Disrespect for your home shows disrespect for your neighbors.

2. *Don't be afraid to try foods that are new to you!*

   a. The students cheer when the cafeteria serves brownies.

   b. Ethnic foods often feature delicious spices.

   c. Burned meat tastes better than undercooked meat.

   d. A very limited menu gets repetitive and boring.

3. *Sports fans are sometimes too "fanatic."*

   a. Thousands of hot dogs are consumed at major league games.

   b. Riots sometimes break out after championship games.

   c. Kids wait outside the park, hoping to catch a home run ball.

   d. Pete goes to the game in spite of his high fever.

B. Use the facts and figures below to write a complete paragraph on the next page. Begin with a well-written topic sentence.

- Babe Ruth played in 10 World Series.

- He played 21 seasons in the American League.

- He held 76 all-time major league records.

- In 1927, Babe Ruth set a record of 60 home runs.

- In his career, he batted 714 home runs.

- He batted in 2,209 runs.

Babe Ruth

TOPIC SENTENCE: _____

PARAGRAPH: _____

_____

_____

_____

_____

_____

C. Write an original paragraph about an imaginary person, place, or thing. Invent *facts and figures* to support your claim that the object of your paragraph is "the very best."

TOPIC SENTENCE: _____ is without a doubt the very best

_____.

PARAGRAPH: _____

_____

_____

_____

_____

_____

D. Suppose you're a hard-working employee who consistently does a great job. Do you deserve a pay raise? Of course you do! Write a paragraph to convince your boss that you've earned a better salary. Use *examples* of your excellent work performance to support your claim.

TOPIC SENTENCE: _____

_____

PARAGRAPH: _____

_____

_____

_____

_____

Lesson 6

Persuasive Paragraphs 2

Every sentence in the body of a paragraph must support the topic sentence. Unnecessary details distract the reader and weaken your message.

EXAMPLE:

A community's library is one of its most valuable resources. The free public library in our town is located at the corner of Fifth and Oak. Public libraries offer all people, rich or poor, access to vital information and great literature. A fee of 25 cents is charged for each day a borrowed book is overdue. Supporting the public library is a wise investment in the citizenry of any and all towns.

A. Find two sentences in the example paragraph that do *not* support the topic sentence. Write them on the lines.

- _____
  _____
- _____
  _____

B. In each paragraph below, cross out the sentence that doesn't belong. Then write an original sentence to replace the one you eliminated. Be sure your new sentence supports the topic sentence.

1. Even a short daily workout can make you a lot healthier. A brisk, 20-minute walk exercises your lungs as well as your leg muscles. Attractive nylon sweatsuits are very popular at health clubs and gyms. Lifting even light weights tones your muscles and increases your body strength.

REPLACEMENT SENTENCE: _____

_____

2. Michael Chu is the best candidate for class president. His good grades set a fine example for other students. His cheerful attitude and courteous manners are important qualifications for leadership. Michael's twin sisters, Rose and Gale, will attend our school next year. I urge all class members to vote for Michael Chu.

REPLACEMENT SENTENCE: _____

_____

Most paragraphs you write are part of longer compositions. Some paragraphs, however, are intended to stand alone. These paragraphs must have a *concluding sentence*. Usually, the concluding sentence summarizes information. It doesn't add new information. It simply repeats the main idea, using different words. For an example, read the concluding sentence in the paragraph about libraries on page 18.

C. Write a concluding sentence for each paragraph below.

1. I strongly believe that space exploration is a big waste of money. Hardworking taxpayers are more interested in affordable housing than they are in what's happening on a distant planet. Parents who can't find jobs aren't primarily concerned about the advancement of science. They're worried about feeding their children.

CONCLUDING SENTENCE: _____

_____

2. Tobacco is the leading cause of preventable deaths in America. Research has conclusively proven that smoking causes lung disease. Pregnant women who smoke put their babies at risk for fetal injury, premature birth, and low birth weight.

CONCLUDING SENTENCE: _____

_____

D. Write an original persuasive paragraph on the lines below. Be sure your paragraph includes a clear topic sentence, several detail sentences, and an appropriate conclusion.

_____

_____

_____

_____

_____

_____

_____

_____

Redundancy

An effective sentence contains only those words necessary to express the main idea. Any words or phrases that do not add to meaning are *redundant*. The best sentences are never too wordy; they are concise and to the point.

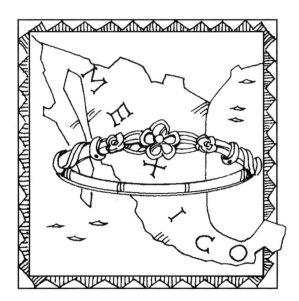

REDUNDANT SENTENCE:

The bracelet which is made of solid silver was made by an artist in Mexico.

CONCISE SENTENCE:

The solid silver bracelet was made by a Mexican artist.

Notice that eliminating extra words makes the sentence easier to read and understand.

A. Read each sentence carefully. Then rewrite it on the line, eliminating repetition and redundancy. *Hint:* Look for unnecessary synonyms or definitions and phrases that can be shortened to one word.

1. School starts at 8:00 A.M. in the morning and ends at 3:00 P.M. in the afternoon.

   _____

2. The little child called Rafael is a preschool student.

   _____

3. Trimming and pruning trees can be done during any season of the year.

   _____

4. The bike that belongs to Henry has a broken chain that must be replaced.

   _____

5. Do you ever think back and reminisce about your former childhood?

   _____

6. A girl who is from Germany lives next door to my house.

   _____

Here are some more examples of redundant wording.

———— REDUNDANT ————		———— CONCISE ————
No one knows the name of the anonymous author.	←→	*The author is anonymous.*
Extra, unnecessary words make sentences clumsy and awkward.	←→	*Unnecessary words make sentences clumsy.*
We decided that we would go to Canada.	←→	*We decided to go to Canada.*
the history of Europe	←→	*European history*

B. Rewrite the sentences, eliminating redundancies. Make every word count!

1. The swimmer who swims the fastest will accept the award with pride.

   _____

2. Use care when you consider each separate answer before you come to a decision and make your choice.

   _____

3. All of the athletes must follow the rules made by Coach Gordon.

   _____

4. In addition, Harold wants to add potato salad to the lunch for the picnic.

   _____

5. The other students in Emily's class voted and elected her as class president.

   _____

6. They agreed that they would go out for some pizza after the game.

   _____

7. The homework which was assigned yesterday is due on Monday, the first day of the school week.

   _____

Lesson
7
Facts and Opinions

Persuasive writing always promotes the writer's judgment or opinion. It's important to be able to recognize the difference between facts and opinions. Unlike a statement of opinion, a statement of fact can be proven right or wrong. *Hint:* Remember that not everyone might agree with an opinion because it can't be proven.

FACTS:

Dogs are popular pets.
Spinach is nutritious.

OPINIONS:

Dogs are more fun than cats.
You should eat more spinach.

A. Write an appropriate statement to complete each pair of statements below.

1. FACT: _____

   OPINION: Paris is the greatest city in the world.

2. FACT: Mount Everest is higher than Mount McKinley.

   OPINION: _____

3. FACT: John F. Kennedy was America's 35th president.

   OPINION: _____

4. FACT: _____

   OPINION: If you like spicy food, you'll love Pedro's chili!

Opinions are often signaled by words that show approval or disapproval. Some of these words are *good, better, bad, best, poor,* and *great.* Words that advise or recommend—such as *should, ought to,* or *must*—are also signals of opinion.

B. Use one of the *italicized* words above in an opinion statement about each subject below.

1. (a new shampoo) _____

   _____

2. (a sporting event) _____

   _____

3. (a popular song) _____

   _____

4. (prom night) _____

   _____

As much as you want to promote your opinion, it's important to be fair. That's why it's a good idea for persuasive writers to *qualify* their statements. Unqualified statements are often unfair.

QUALIFIED STATEMENTS:

Men usually require more food than women.

Some old people are dangerous drivers.

UNQUALIFIED STATEMENTS:

Men require more food than women.

Old people are dangerous drivers.

C. Use the qualifying words in the box—or any others you know—to rewrite the following sentences as fair statements of opinion.

almost	in my opinion	it seems	some
most	apparently	several	many
I think	supposedly	seems to	often
might	sometimes	probably	may

1. Flooding will occur if the rain doesn't stop soon.

   _____

2. Citizens are unhappy with the governor's performance.

   _____

3. The death penalty is unjust and inhumane.

   _____

4. Victoria was the greatest queen in English history.

   _____

5. Lilacs have a sweeter scent than roses.

   _____

6. Migraine headaches are caused by stress.

   _____

7. That face cream makes wrinkles disappear overnight.

   _____

8. Voters are suspicious of that candidate's record.

   _____

Lesson 8

Letters to the Editor

Have you noticed that newspaper articles are grouped by category? World news and local news are usually in different sections. The same is true for sports news and comic strips. One very important part of the paper is the editorial, or opinion, section. Here, right alongside nationally known columnists, everyday readers can "have their say." This part of the editorial page is often called *Letters to the Editor*.

EXAMPLE:

LETTERS TO THE EDITOR

Dear Editor:

I strongly object to the *Daily Drone*'s coverage of the recent Potatoheads concert at Marshall Park. Obviously, the big crowd of cheering spudbuds (as faithful fans are called) didn't agree with your reviewer's opinion. Either he doesn't understand the new rhythms of technosqueal or the man is tone-deaf! Give us a break! The next time the Potatoheads are in town, send an open-minded reviewer!

A. Scan the Letters to the Editor in your local newspaper. Then write **T** or **F** to show whether each statement below is *true* or *false*.

1. _____ Many readers share their favorite recipes in letters to the editor.

2. _____ Letters to the editor are usually quite short.

3. _____ These days, letters to the editor are often sent in by fax and e-mail.

4. _____ Readers' letters that disagree with the newspaper's opinions are never published.

5. _____ Readers' letters are sometimes reactions to articles that have been published in the newspaper.

6. _____ Letters to the editor are often examples of persuasive writing.

7. _____ You must be at least 18 years old to get your letter published in the newspaper.

8. _____ It's a good idea to phone the newspaper every day to find out when your letter will appear.

9. _____ A letter about a lost dog would not be appropriate in the Letters to the Editor section.

10. _____ A newspaper editor will usually correct minor spelling errors in the letters it publishes.

B. Suppose *you* are the editor of the *Readers Speak Out* section. You receive as many as 100 letters a day, but you can publish only 10! How do you decide which to print and which to leave out? First, read each of the sample letters. Decide whether or not to publish it. Then explain why or why not.

LETTER 1

Dear Editor,

I seen your dum, dum advise for voters last weak. Throw them bumbs out of office! Y knot wreckomend me, I.M.A. Crackpot!

---

1. Consider for publication? ☐ **YES** ☐ **NO**

   Why or why not? _____

   _____

   _____

   _____

LETTER 2

Dear Editor,

My whole family was offended by the photo of a naked dog on the front page. For shame! Have you no decency? Please cancel our subscription.

---

2. Consider for publication? ☐ **YES** ☐ **NO**

   Why or why not? _____

   _____

   _____

   _____

LETTER 3

Dear Editor,

Why should big businesses get more tax breaks than ordinary citizens do? I say it's time to stand up for the average taxpayer and vote NO on Proposition 99.

---

3. Consider for publication? ☐ **YES** ☐ **NO**

   Why or why not? _____

   _____

   _____

   _____

C. Now write your own letter to the editor. Make sure your topic is appropriate, and offer at least one reason to support your opinion.

Dear Editor,

_____

_____

_____

_____

_____

_____

_____

_____

Lesson 9 — Movie Review

Many newspapers, magazines, and TV stations hire professional reviewers to "prescreen" new movies. Why? To guide their readers and viewers as to which new films are worth seeing—and which are not.

The reviewer has a threefold job: to inform, to evaluate, and to recommend. Some reviewers use a form like the one below to jot down basic information and their initial impressions.

CRITIC'S CHOICE

It is this critic's opinion that sequels should *never* be made. But there's always an <u>exception to the rule</u>!

★★★☆☆ *Arachnid-Man 1*

★★★★☆ *Arachnid-Man 2*

★★★★★ *Arachnid-Man 3*

————INFORMATION————

What? _____
(NAME OF MOVIE)

What kind? _____
(MUSICAL, MYSTERY, SCI FI, ETC.)

Who? _____
(THE MOVIE'S STARS)

_____   _____
(THE DIRECTOR)   (THE AUTHOR, IF ADAPTED FROM A BOOK)

When? _____
(DATE MOVIE OPENS)

————EVALUATION————

Plot _____
(GRIPPING/EXCITING, ETC. —OR— CONFUSING/WEAK, ETC.)

Characters _____
(BELIEVABLE/CHARMING, ETC. —OR— UNREALISTIC/WOODEN, ETC.)

Dialogue _____
(CLEVER/SNAPPY, ETC. —OR— STILTED/OUTLANDISH, ETC.)

Sets/Locations _____
(TRUE-TO-LIFE/SPECTACULAR, ETC. —OR— FAKE/BORING, ETC.)

Wardrobe/Makeup _____
(TRENDY, EXQUISITE, ETC. —OR— INAPPROPRIATE, ODD, ETC.)

Special Effects _____
(BREATHTAKING, ETC. —OR— NOT APPLICABLE —OR— SAME OLD, SAME OLD, ETC.)

Details Worth Mentioning _____

_____

_____

_____
(SPECIFIC EXAMPLES OF WHAT YOU LOVED OR HATED ABOUT THE FILM)

————RECOMMENDATION————

Rate with one to five stars, from worst to best: ★   ★   ★   ★   ★

A. Think of a movie you saw quite recently. If you haven't seen a movie in a while, review any movie that made a strong impression on you, one way or another. Perhaps it's a much-loved classic you've seen again and again. Or maybe it's a horror movie that scared you silly! All that matters is that you remember it well and have strong feelings about it. Use the form on page 26 to make notes for a movie review.

B. Use the notes you wrote on page 26 to help you write a complete movie review on the lines below.

1. Begin by writing a catchy title or headline for your review.

2. Your first paragraph should name the movie, and present your opinion of it in a way that captures your readers' attention.

3. Your second, or middle, paragraph should contain descriptive details and examples that support your opinion.

4. Your third, or concluding, paragraph should summarize your review, rephrase your opinion, and make a recommendation to your readers.

Title: _____

(1) _____

_____

_____

_____

(2) _____

_____

_____

_____

(3) _____

_____

_____

_____

Frequently Confused Words

A. Read the definition and example sentence for each word. Then demonstrate correct usage by writing example sentences of your own.

can physically able
Joe can do pushups.

may implies permission
You may leave early.

1. (can) _____

2. (may) _____

lie to recline
Lie down for a rest.

lay to place
Lay the shirt in the box.

3. (lie) _____

4. (lay) _____

sit take a seat
Sit on the green chair.

set to place
Set the vase on the mantel.

5. (sit) _____

6. (set) _____

loan something lent, especially money
Thanks for the loan.

lend to give something or the use of something for a while
He will lend her his car.

7. (loan) _____

8. (lend) _____

leave to go away from
They are about to leave.

let to permit or allow
Let the boys go outdoors.

9. (leave) _____

10. (let) _____

B. One word or two? Complete each sentence with the correct word in parentheses. Check a dictionary if you're not sure of spellings or word meanings.

(all together / altogether)

1. The brothers and sisters were

   _____ for the

   holidays.

2. Laurie was _____

   disgusted by the odor of the

   rotting garbage.

(every one / everyone)

3. _____ at work

   agreed with my suggestion.

4. The greedy children ate

   _____ of

   the raisin cookies.

(all ready / already)

5. The Cub Scouts were

   _____

   to leave for camp.

6. Long before the box office

   opened, people were

   _____

   waiting in line.

(some time / sometime)

7. Won't you come to visit us

   _____ soon?

8. He needs _____

   to get used to the idea.

C. Circle the word that correctly completes each sentence. Check a dictionary if you're not sure!

1. The new president's (social / sociable) programs include plans to help the aged and the mentally ill.

2. Jack's big yawn (inferred / implied) that he was bored with the lecture.

3. How much (further / farther) do we still have to walk?

4. Be sure to (bring / take) a raincoat when you go out tonight.

Lesson 10

Working World 1

Most people look for new jobs many times in their lives. Did you realize that job-hunting often calls for some persuasive writing? Perhaps you want to respond to a job ad. Or maybe you want to get a job at a certain store or office in town. In both cases, a well-written business letter is an appropriate way to introduce yourself.

A letter to a potential employer should include the following four elements:

1. the name of the position or type of work that interests you

2. a description of your educational background and availability

3. a short summary of your experience and qualifications

4. an offer of references and a request for an interview

A. Suppose you're interested in an ad for a summer job as a recreation aide at a city park. The ad instructs you to respond by letter to Ms. Louise Haines, Parks and Recreation Dept., Cromwell, CA 97001. Complete the business letter format below with a letter of application. Make sure to include all four elements. Remember that your goal is to impress the employer enough to call you in for an interview.

B. Put yourself in the place of an employer. His or her goal is to fill the job opening with a qualified person—usually as soon as possible. Perhaps the employer has dozens of application letters to evaluate. But there's only enough time to interview two or three job candidates! Which letters would be easiest to eliminate? From the employer's point of view, circle the words that correctly complete each sentence.

1. The tone of an effective application letter is (chummy / friendly) yet (businesslike / demanding).

2. An employer may not take time to read a letter that is too (short / long) or (informative / messy).

3. A proper business letter should be written on (plain white / fancy floral) paper.

4. Being very careful with accurate spelling and punctuation shows (nervousness / effort).

Some experts recommend following up a job interview with a letter to the employer. The purpose of such a letter is to: (1) thank the interviewer for his or her time; (2) express a sincere interest in the job; and (3) add any information you may have forgotten to give in the interview.

C. Read the example follow-up letter closely. Then rewrite it on the lines. Correct any errors you find, and change the wording as necessary.

Dear Ms. Gomez,

    It was good for you to meet me. I appreseheeate your time. I'll dew a grate job if you higher me as a camp counselor.

    Oh, I forgot to tell you that my best friend is allso a counselor at your camp. He hopes I get hired so we can goof off together.

    When do I start? Call me after 8 tonight.

       Your pal,

_____ :

_____

_____

_____

_____

_____

_____

_____

_____

_____

_____

_____ ,

Lesson 11

Working World 2

At some time in your life, a friend, coworker, or former employee may ask you for a letter of reference. In this important communication, you will recommend someone for employment based on your knowledge of that person's character and abilities. Strong references can convince an employer to select one applicant out of many.

A. Put yourself in the place of an employer who's reading reference letters. What key qualities will help you decide to hire a certain applicant? What qualities are *not* relevant or useful? Circle six key qualities.

popular	hardworking	short	shy
reliable	cooperative	playful	chubby
young	determined	energetic	honest

B. A one-time fellow employee asks you for a reference letter. Use your imagination to help you fill in the blanks of the letter below. Without going overboard, make your former coworker sound as impressive as you can.

To Whom It May Concern:

I have known _____ for _____ years. We worked
(NAME)   (NUMBER)

together at _____ from _____ to _____. Our job
(NAME OF COMPANY)   (DATE)   (DATE)

entailed _____.
(JOB DESCRIPTION)

During our long association, I came to know _____ as
(NAME)

_____, _____, and _____.
(ADJECTIVE)   (ADJECTIVE)   (ADJECTIVE)

I have never known him/her to _____, _____,
(VERB)   (VERB)

or _____. His/Her most outstanding characteristic is probably
(VERB)

his/her _____.
(PHRASE)

He/She never stops trying to _____.
(PHRASE)

I am very pleased to recommend _____
(NAME)

for employment at your company.

Sincerely,

_____
(YOUR NAME)

C. You're planning to apply for a really great job. You've asked a former boss or teacher to write a letter recommending you. What skills, accomplishments, and personal qualities would you most want to be mentioned? *Hint:* Try to see yourself through the eyes of a future employer.

SKILLS:

a. _____

b. _____

c. _____

ACCOMPLISHMENTS:

a. _____

b. _____

c. _____

PERSONAL QUALITIES:

a. _____

b. _____

c. _____

D. Now write a letter of recommendation for yourself. Draw on the details listed above. Add any other information you think would make a good impression.

_____

_____

_____

_____

_____

_____

_____

_____

_____

_____

Sincerely,

_____

Lesson 12

Working World 3

The ability to express yourself persuasively can serve you very well in the workplace. Communication on the job is extremely important. Consider the following situation:

You have a good idea for improving your workplace.
How can you convince the boss to make the change?

One good way to communicate in the workplace is to write a memorandum, or *memo*. An effective memo is short and to the point. It presents facts rather than feelings; in other words, it is businesslike in tone.

A. Write a memo explaining your idea to an imaginary boss. Fill in the traditional, three-part format below. Invent any examples you need to support your recommendation. (Remember to double-check your spelling and punctuation!)

Date: _____ (TODAY'S DATE)

To: _____ (BOSS'S NAME)

From: _____ (YOUR NAME)

Re: _____ (THE TOPIC OF YOUR MEMO)

(STATEMENT OF PURPOSE) _____

_____

_____

(DESCRIPTION OF PROBLEM OR SITUATION) _____

_____

_____

_____

_____

(RECOMMENDATION) _____

_____

_____

_____

_____

_____

Thank you for your attention.

B. Now consider another reason for writing a memo. Suppose you've been working at the same job for two years. You've learned a lot and performed very well. How can you convince your boss that you've earned a pay raise?

Write a memo on the lines below. Before you begin, think about your request from the *boss*'s viewpoint. (Your personal needs and wishes are of less importance to the boss than your value to the company!)

Date: _____ (TODAY'S DATE)

To: _____ (BOSS'S NAME)

From: _____ (YOUR NAME)

Re: _____ (THE TOPIC OF YOUR MEMO)

(STATEMENT OF PURPOSE) _____

_____

_____

(SUPPORTING FACTS/EXAMPLES)_____

_____

_____

_____

_____

(RECOMMENDATION)_____

_____

_____

_____

_____

_____

Thank you for your attention.

C. Now write three statements you should *not* make in your memo requesting a pay raise.

1. _____

2. _____

3. _____

Capitalization

The following items should always be capitalized:

- **the first word in a sentence**
  An X-ray will be required.

- **names of persons, places, streets, and organizations**

  Sandra Day O'Connor   *Paris, France*
  Oak Street   *The United Nations*

- **the first word in a direct quotation**   *"We're hungry!" the children shouted.*

- **names of languages, specific school courses, documents, and important historical events**

  Spanish   *Advanced Algebra*   *Emancipation Proclamation*   *Civil War*

A. Rewrite the sentences, adding or deleting capital letters as necessary.

1. during world war II, many Citizens of Europe went hungry.

   _____

2. Have You tried the new greek restaurant on Tenth avenue?

   _____

3. Martin said, "this school doesn't offer many History Courses."

   _____

4. The internal Revenue service collects Federal Taxes.

   _____

5. The Headquarters of the American cancer society has been relocated.

   _____

6. Paul studies Government at Marshall high school in chicago.

   _____

7. his Brother and Sister live with their dad on grand Boulevard.

   _____

Here are some more examples of words that should always be capitalized.

- **days of the week, months, and holidays**

  Tuesday
  July 4
  Independence Day

- **the first word and each important word in the title of a book, play, poem, etc.**

  A Tree Grows in Brooklyn

- **certain abbreviations**

  M.D.
  NAACP

- **the initials of a person's name**

  John Q. Public
  T. J. Ackerley

- **a personal title only when it comes before the name**

  General Grant
  Uncle Vanya

- **proper adjectives**

  Congressional
  Constitutional

B. Rewrite the sentences, adding capital letters as necessary.

1. my uncle was a sergeant in the u.s. army.

   _____

2. gone with the wind will be screened at 2:10 P.M.

   _____

3. dr. joseph mckenna, d.d.s., opened his office in may.

   _____

4. sir lawrence olivier was a brilliant english actor.

   _____

5. no one recognized aunt polly in her clever halloween costume.

   _____

6. grace m. johnson, a professor, earned her ph.d. at indiana university.

   _____

7. I read "the charge of the light brigade" in my british literature class.

   _____

Lesson 13 — Advertising 1

Companies spend a lot of money to develop new products. Often, they spend even *more* money to promote those products to consumers. Advertising is big business.

The spoken or written words used in ads are called *ad copy*. You've probably noticed that ad copy is usually a blend of fact and opinion.

EXAMPLES:

FACT	OPINION
20% off *every* item in the store! **Guaranteed satisfaction or your money back!**	**We offer the friendliest service in town!** **Magic Makeup will make *you* feel like a movie star!**

A. Think about your favorite soap, toothpaste, or hair care product. Then imagine that you're a copywriter assigned to write an ad. Begin brainstorming ideas by listing two facts and two opinions about that product.

FACT: _____

FACT: _____

OPINION: _____

OPINION: _____

B. What claims can you make that would encourage consumers to try a certain product? Specifically, in what ways does it stand out from other products of its kind? For example, is it less expensive, easier to use, or does it have a unique "extra ingredient"? Is the packaging (tube, bottle, jar, etc.) especially well-designed or attractive?

Product Comparisons

Why is _____ distinctly different? Unlike
                (PRODUCT NAME)

other _____, it always _____,
          (PRODUCT TYPE)   (POSITIVE RESULT)

and never _____. You'll also appreciate its
              (NEGATIVE RESULT)

_____ and _____.
   (PRODUCT FEATURE)   (PRODUCT FEATURE)

If you want _____ _____,
                (ADJECTIVE)   (SKIN, TEETH, OR HAIR)

you'll be glad you tried _____.
                              (PRODUCT NAME)

Adjectives (describing words) play a very important role in ad copy. Clever copywriters are very careful when they choose words to describe a product. To persuade consumers to buy, they use only words that create a positive image.

C. Rewrite the following lines of ad copy by replacing the negative words with positive ones. Select words from the box—or any other words you know—that create a positive image.

buttery	elite	supreme	cozy
brilliant	firm	thrifty	glow
ambitious	crisp	sturdy	snug

1. Pretentious cars for pretentious people

   _____

2. Cramped seaside cottage available for summer rental

   _____

3. Brittle, fatty-flavored fried chicken

   _____

4. The glare from our new light bulb is absolutely blinding!

   _____

5. Cheap shoppers will appreciate our low, low prices.

   _____

D. Adjectives aren't the only words that impact consumer reaction. Now rewrite the ad copy below, using different *verbs* (action words).

1. Spring Morning perfume reeks like fresh lilacs.

   _____

2. GoodGargle mouthwash is guaranteed to scrub your breath.

   _____

3. Hoard your money in an account at BigBucks Bank.

   _____

Lesson 14

Advertising 2

Many advertisements overcome sales resistance by appealing to feelings rather than rational thoughts. That's why copywriters like to associate their products with appealing *sensory images*.

EXAMPLES: *Heal-Quick Lip Balm feels great. It makes even chapped lips break out in a big smile.*

Do you like the fragrance of fresh spring flowers? You'll love the scent of Sudso Detergent!

A. Write a line of ad copy for each product below. Associate each product with an attractive sensory image. As an example, the first one has been done for you.

TASTE

1. a mouthwash *tingles your taste buds with minty freshness*
2. peanut butter _____

TOUCH

3. a bed pillow _____
4. talcum powder _____

SMELL

5. shampoo _____
6. scented candle _____

SOUND

7. a car engine _____
8. a CD player _____

LOOK

9. a diamond ring _____
10. an HDTV screen _____

Many ads use colorful figures of speech called *similes* to capture interest. These imaginative expressions always contain the words "like" or "as."

EXAMPLES: Spots-No-More Carpet Cleaner *works like a charm.*
It removes the worst stains *as quick as a wink.*

B. Read the similes below. What kind of product does each simile bring to mind? Think of a clever name for that product. Then write a line of ad copy that contains the simile. The first one has been done for you as an example.

1. *as quiet as a whisper* _Unlike other powerful vacuum cleaners,_

_____

2. *sparkles like diamonds* _____

_____

3. *as fresh as a daisy* _____

_____

4. *fits like a glove* _____

_____

5. *as light as a feather* _____

_____

6. *feels like velvet* _____

_____

C. Now try writing ad copy on your own. Remember that your objective is to persuade consumers to *buy*. Follow the directions.

1. Write two statements about a certain brand of bread. (Make up the brand name.) Use a *fact* in one statement and an *opinion* in the other.

a. _____

_____

b. _____

_____

2. Write ad copy for a new brand of paper towels. Compare your towels to other brands, using at least three words or phrases that will make your towels seem better.

_____

_____

_____

_____

_____

Lesson
15   Letter of Complaint

Many ads aren't completely truthful. Perhaps they list a wrong price or show a product doing something it cannot do. This is called *false advertising*.

You can complain about such ads. Consumer rights are protected by agencies of the federal and state governments. Their numbers are listed under *Consumer Protection* in the telephone book's white pages. You can also complain directly, in person or in writing, to the store where you bought the item.

How can you make your letter persuasive? Support your complaint with convincing facts, reasons, and examples.

A. Read the items below. On the first line after each item, support your complaint with a convincing reason, fact, or example. On the second line, explain how you would like the problem to be solved.

1. Your ad announced a "storewide sale," but only a few items were discounted.

   _____

   _____

2. Your spot remover ate a hole in my best suit jacket.

   _____

   _____

3. The "juicy red" strawberries described in your ad were green and as hard as rocks.

   _____

   _____

4. Many clerks at your store know nothing about the merchandise.

   _____

   _____

5. I'm not at all satisfied with your carpet cleaning services.

   _____

   _____

6. The "fast, friendly" service you advertise is neither fast nor friendly.

   _____

   _____

B. A letter of complaint is a formal business letter. No matter how upset you are, your tone must be respectful. Ranting and raving are *not* persuasive forms of communication. Rewrite the following lines from an angry letter of complaint. Create a different tone by expressing the same thought in different words. The first one has been done for you as an example.

1. I demand that you fire the jerk who was so rude to me.

   I strongly suggest that you give your employees more training in courteous customer service.

2. You'd better refund my money immediately—or else.

   _____

   _____

3. Your Mighty Muscle Treadmill is a piece of junk!

   _____

   _____

C. On the lines below, write an effective letter of complaint about a product or service—real or imaginary—that disappointed you. Use specific facts and examples, and be sure that the tone of your letter is businesslike and respectful.

Connotation and Denotation

Did you know that all words have both *connotations* and *denotations*? A word's dictionary meaning is its denotation. Connotation refers to the attitudes and feelings the word suggests. Words with similar dictionary definitions can have very different connotations.

Persuasive writers choose words carefully. They make sure the connotations of their key words support their point of view.

POSITIVE	NEGATIVE
thrifty	cheap
proud	haughty
slim	skinny
unique	eccentric

A. In each item below, think about the viewpoint the writer wishes to promote. Circle the word that correctly completes each sentence.

1. You're writing a campaign speech for a candidate who is unusually frank and honest. You describe the candidate as (plainspoken / blunt).

2. You're writing ad copy for an expensive necklace. You describe the necklace as (flimsy / delicate).

3. You're writing an essay about a historical figure you admire. You describe her personality as (unsociable / shy).

4. You're writing a newspaper editorial urging that a new sports stadium be built in your town. You describe citizen support as (enthusiastic / fanatic).

B. Draw lines to match negative and positive connotations of words with similar meanings.

1. argue   a. eavesdrop

2. hoodwink   b. annoy

3. flatter   c. coerce

4. convince   d. fight

5. overhear   e. compliment

6. tease   f. outwit

C. Choose one *negative* and one *positive* word from the box to match the **boldface** word in each sentence. As an example, the first one has been done for you.

daring	meticulous	suspicious	reckless
wary	assertive	persistent	fussy
playful	revolutionary	aggressive	unproven
classic	stubborn	outdated	silly

1. She was very **precise** about how she wanted the items to be displayed.

   POSITIVE: _____*meticulous*_____   NEGATIVE: _____*fussy*_____

2. He kept his **old** roadster in immaculate condition.

   POSITIVE: _____   NEGATIVE: _____

3. The mayor's **new** proposal could make some dramatic changes in city government.

   POSITIVE: _____   NEGATIVE: _____

4. Ryan's **mischievous** behavior delights students and annoys teachers.

   POSITIVE: _____   NEGATIVE: _____

5. Alexis was quite **insistent** when she asked her boss for a raise.

   POSITIVE: _____   NEGATIVE: _____

6. Until you consider all the facts, it's best to be **guarded** before making an important decision.

   POSITIVE: _____   NEGATIVE: _____

7. Clete was **unwavering** in his search for an answer to the difficult problem.

   POSITIVE: _____   NEGATIVE: _____

8. That gymnast's **bold** leap was unlike anything we've ever seen before.

   POSITIVE: _____   NEGATIVE: _____

Lesson 16   Public Service Appeal

There are many "good causes" that need and deserve the public's support. Suppose you've been hired as a publicist or fundraiser for one of these causes. Today your task is to write ads for newspapers and magazines.

A. After each "good cause" below, write three persuasive sentences that will encourage readers to lend their support. *Hint:* Use colorful examples and descriptions.

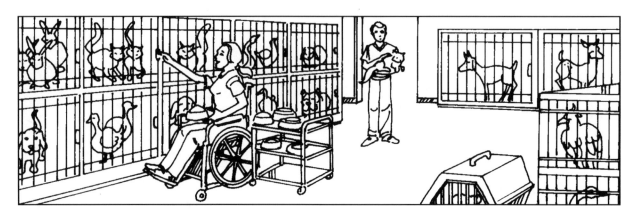

1. *Adopt a pet at the animal rescue center!*

   a. _____

   b. _____

   c. _____

2. *Donate clean, usable clothing to the homeless shelter!*

   a. _____

   b. _____

   c. _____

3. *Volunteer as a tutor at your local elementary school!*

   a. _____

   b. _____

   c. _____

4. *Give blood at the American Red Cross Blood Center!*

   a. _____

   b. _____

   c. _____

5. *Send $30.00 a month to "adopt" a young war orphan!*

   a. _____

   b. _____

   c. _____

6. *Donate turkeys for Thanksgiving baskets for needy families!*

   a. _____

   b. _____

   c. _____

7. *Help us clean up the neighborhood playground this weekend!*

   a. _____

   b. _____

   c. _____

B. Clever writers make an effort to overcome their audience's resistance to public service appeals. Read the typical excuses given for not responding to a call for help. After each one, write a persuasive statement that effectively contradicts that argument. As an example, the first one has been done for you.

1. "My small contribution won't make much of a dent in such a big problem."

   Give only what you can afford—small donations add up! If we all pull together, we can make a big difference!

2. "It's too much trouble to drive all the way downtown just to deliver a bag of used clothes."

   _____

   _____

3. "I'd like to tutor, but I'm probably too old (or too young)."

   _____

   _____

4. "I'm already pretty busy, so I can't spare much time."

   _____

   _____

Lesson 17

Personal Letters 1

You'll be able to use your persuasive writing skills on many occasions in your personal life. Before you begin to write, remind yourself of the guidelines you've learned so far in this book.

- **Prewrite by brainstorming ideas and taking notes.**
  It's always a good idea to jot down your thoughts before you write. Even brief notes help you focus on the task at hand. Notes also remind you to include all important details.

- **Consider your audience.**
  Are you writing to a pal, someone you don't know, or your grandmother? Your word choice and tone will usually change with your audience.

- **Support your message with reasons, examples, or facts.**
  Use all the supporting details you can to make your message sound reasonable and worthy of consideration.

- **Make your "reason for writing" very clear and straightforward.**
  Don't "bury" the purpose of your letter in paragraphs of idle chitchat. Make your main point easy for the reader to identify.

- **Take the time to proofread and rewrite as necessary.**
  Check your sentences for weak word choice, punctuation errors, and unnecessary words. A letter that reflects your very best work shows respect for the reader.

A. The following note of apology was written by a schoolboy to one of his neighbors. Think about the guidelines stated above. Then write an improved version of the letter on page 49.

Mrs. Henderson,

I'm the guy who smashed your window yesterday. My mom says you're realy steamed at me. That's why she's makeing me right this letter.

I told her the ball I hit threw your window was a home run! But did she congradgulate me? No weigh! It's just a peace of glass. A knew window pain won't cost you much. And hey—it was an aksident! Give me a brake!

Your niehbor,
Lefty Louis

P.S. When can I get my ball back?

_____ ,

_____

_____

_____

_____

_____

_____

_____

_____

_____

_____

_____

_____ ,

_____

B. Imagine you're a college freshman, living away from home for the first time. Unexpected expenses have depleted your monthly spending allowance—in just one week! On the lines below, write a letter to your parents requesting more money. Use persuasive facts and examples to convince them that your request is reasonable.

_____ ,

_____

_____

_____

_____

_____

_____

_____

_____

_____

_____

_____ ,

_____

Lesson 18 Personal Letters 2

A. You're eager to attend a highly respected summer wrestling camp at a major university. You wish your best friend and fellow wrestler Todd could go with you. If only Todd hadn't moved away last year! Write a letter urging him to join you at the camp. To be convincing, list as many benefits as possible. Make it easy for Todd to say yes!

_____ ,

_____

_____

_____

_____

_____

_____

_____

_____

_____ ,

_____

B. Congratulations! You've won a scholarship to a fine college. But you can't afford to pay for room and board. Your elderly, widowed grandma lives near the college. Will she let you move in with her? Write her a letter, proposing your idea. Offer several good reasons to support your plan. *Hint:* Grandma would probably enjoy your company as well as your help around the house.

_____ ,

_____

_____

_____

_____

_____

_____

_____

_____ ,

_____

C. You're away at college when your mom calls. She says your younger brother seems to be running wild! He's skipping school, staying out late, and being disrespectful to her. She asks you to write him a letter setting him straight. Your brother has always looked up to you. How can you encourage him to change his ways? Write your letter on the lines.

_____,

_____

_____

_____

_____

_____

_____

_____

_____

_____,

_____

D. You and your sister get into an angry shouting match at a big family party. The guests are shocked and your parents are embarrassed. Feeling ashamed, you beg your parents' forgiveness. Then you write an apology to your sister. Your letter includes a plan for avoiding such confrontations in the future.

_____,

_____

_____

_____

_____

_____

_____

_____

_____,

_____

Verbs: Agreement with Subject

No doubt you already know that singular subjects take singular verbs and plural subjects take plural verbs.

SINGULAR: *Lance is a Democrat.*
A fly buzzes.

PLURAL: *The Hongs are Republicans.*
The flies buzz.

But some cases of subject-verb agreement can cause problems. Here are two examples:

COLLECTIVE NOUNS:

• Does a collective noun indicate a group acting together as a single unit? Use a singular verb.

The jury has brought in a verdict.

• Does the collective noun indicate members of a group acting individually? Use a plural verb.

The jury were arguing among themselves.

NOUNS OF MEASUREMENT:

• Does the noun name an amount of money or a measurement that refers to a sum or a whole amount? Use a singular verb.

Fifty dollars is the amount that he still owes.

• Does the measurement or amount refer to a number of individual units? Use a plural verb.

Fifty dollars have been identified as counterfeit.

A. Circle the verb that correctly completes each sentence.

1. Our football team (compete / comp against 10 opponents this year.

2. Ten miles (is / are) a lot of miles to walk without stopping.

3. Twelve dozen packets (is / are) packed in every gross.

4. The committee (were / was) unanimous in its opinion.

5. The band (differ / differs) in their opinions of the new uniforms.

6. One hundred twenty-eight pounds (are / is) Miranda's ideal weight.

Indefinite pronouns—words such as *each, some, nobody,* and *either*—do *not* refer to particular persons or things. These pronouns may be singular or plural, depending on how they are used.

SINGULAR			PLURAL	SINGULAR OR PLURAL	
anybody	everybody	nobody	both	all	none
anyone	everyone	no one	few	any	some
each	one	somebody	many	most	
either	neither	someone	several		

Three pronouns are often mistakenly used as plurals: *each, either,* and *neither*. These pronouns are always singular and take singular verbs.

B. First, circle the verb that agrees with each subject. Then, use each indefinite pronoun in a sentence of your own. Be sure that the verb agrees!

1. Many (applies / apply), but few (are / is) hired.

   _____

2. Some of our class time (is / are) always wasted by disruptions.

   _____

3. Most of our school's athletes (takes / take) their training very seriously.

   _____

4. All of the candidates (have / has) five minutes to speak.

   _____

5. Any supplies that are left over (is / are) stored in that cabinet.

   _____

6. All the maple syrup (have / has) been emptied from the bottle.

   _____

7. Neither of Mr. Cranston's boys (are / is) allowed out after dark.

   _____

Lesson 19

Debate 1: Pros and Cons

There are two sides to most issues. Debaters try to convince the reader or listener to accept one point of view and reject the other. Whether you're arguing *for* or *against* an idea, there are almost always valid points to be made.

Effective argumentation requires solid, believable evidence. You can support your opinion by using facts, examples, contrasts, comparisons, or analogies.

A. Identify each argument by writing *fact*, *example*, *contrast*, *comparison*, or *analogy*.

1. _____ Unlike his brash, outspoken opponent, Mr. Uppington is a courteous gentleman.

2. _____ Only 16 people died in train accidents last year, while 23,500 were killed in automobile crashes.

3. _____ Nutritious foods such as broccoli and beans ensure the good health of vegetarians.

4. _____ Encouragement pays off: Praise is to punishment as a carrot is to a stick.

5. _____ Ms. Crawford is the smartest and most experienced of all the candidates.

In a debate, the idea or premise put forward for discussion is called a *proposition*.

EXAMPLES:
  Most advertisements are full of lies.
  A serious student studies at least two hours a day.

B. Write your own opinion statement, or proposition, about each of the following topics:

1. *animal rights* _____

_____

2. *television* _____

_____

3. *fast food restaurants* _____

_____

4. *tanning salons* _____

_____

C. Write one reasonable argument *for* and one reasonable argument *against* each proposition below. Remember to support your position with a fact, an example, a contrast, a comparison, or an analogy.

1. *Professional athletes are grossly overpaid.*

   PRO _____   CON _____
   _____   _____
   _____   _____
   _____   _____

2. *There is no such thing as a justifiable war.*

   PRO _____   CON _____
   _____   _____
   _____   _____
   _____   _____

3. *Scientists should be allowed to experiment with human cloning.*

   PRO _____   CON _____
   _____   _____
   _____   _____
   _____   _____

4. *Most environmentalists are kooky "tree-huggers."*

   PRO _____   CON _____
   _____   _____
   _____   _____
   _____   _____

5. *Wealthy defendants have an unfair advantage in U.S. courts of law.*

   PRO _____   CON _____
   _____   _____
   _____   _____

6. *Nursery school is a poor substitute for a stay-at-home mom.*

   PRO _____   CON _____
   _____   _____
   _____   _____

Lesson 20

Debate 2: Developing an Argument

A. Read the following debate propositions. Put a check mark (✓) in the *pro* or *con* box to show where you stand. Then write three effective arguments to support your position. Remember to use facts and examples.

PRO CON

1. ☐ ☐ *Speed limits on state highways are unreasonably low.*

a. _____

_____

b. _____

_____

c. _____

_____

PRO CON

2. ☐ ☐ *Both young women and young men should register for military service.*

a. _____

_____

b. _____

_____

c. _____

_____

PRO CON

3. ☐ ☐ *Immigrants to the U.S. should be required to learn and speak English.*

a. _____

_____

b. _____

_____

c. _____

_____

PRO CON

4. ☐ ☐ *Repeat drunk drivers should lose their driver's licenses permanently.*

a. _____

_____

b. _____

_____

c. _____

_____

B. Skillful debaters often conclude their presentations with a dramatic story. The most powerful stories are based on personal experience or the experience of an acquaintance. Write a proposition based on one of the topics in the box or on a topic of your own choosing. Then tell the story on the lines below. Be sure your story supports your argument and concludes your presentation convincingly.

legalized gambling	police abuse of power	drug abuse	equal rights for women

PROPOSITION: _____

_____

STORY: _____

_____

_____

_____

_____

_____

_____

_____

_____

_____

_____

_____

_____

_____

Lesson
21

Candidate's Speech

Imagine that you're running for a seat on the local school board. As a young person, you plan to base your campaign speech on your fresh new ideas for change. Your opponent is an older person with years of experience. His vision of the "ideal school" is quite different from yours. Both of you have valid points to make, and both of you have the same goal: to convince voters that you are the best candidate!

A. Write reasonable "position statements" for both you and your opponent on the following topics.

  1. TOPIC: **How can potential dropouts be encouraged to stay in school?**

     YOU: _____   YOUR OPPONENT: _____

     _____   _____

     _____   _____

  2. TOPIC: **Would students benefit from *more* homework, or *less* homework?**

     YOU: _____   YOUR OPPONENT: _____

     _____   _____

     _____   _____

  3. TOPIC: **Should student government be given more power?**

     YOU: _____   YOUR OPPONENT: _____

     _____   _____

     _____   _____

B. Bad news! Next year, the schools in your district face big budget cuts! In your opinion, what program or activity in the box should be trimmed down to save money? Write your suggestion—and your reasons for making it—on the lines below.

the science club	art classes	the computer lab	choir and orchestra	the sports program

PROGRAM/ACTIVITY TO TRIM: _____

SUPPORT FOR YOUR CHOICE: _____

_____

_____

_____

_____

_____

C. After a candidate's speech, members of the audience are usually given a chance to ask questions. If you are well-prepared, you have studied the issues and made notes in advance. Explain your stand on each issue raised by answering the following questions. Don't forget that your goal is to get votes! Answer every question as respectfully and persuasively as you can.

1. QUESTION: *I learned important skills in my metal and wood shop classes at school. My son's school has eliminated most vocational training. Don't you think that's a big mistake?*

    ANSWER: I (do / do not) support adding more vocational courses to the curriculum because _____

    _____

    _____

2. QUESTION: *My daughter says that cell phones are forbidden in her school. That doesn't seem fair! What's your position on students taking cell phones to school?*

    ANSWER: I (do / do not) think that students should bring cell phones to school because _____

    _____

    _____

3. QUESTION: *The high schools in our district are no longer open campuses. What harm does it do to allow students to have lunch wherever they want to?*

    ANSWER: I (do / do not) support open campuses because _____

    _____

    _____

    _____

4. QUESTION: *I've heard that parents may be fined if their kids skip school a lot. Do you agree with this idea?*

    ANSWER: I (do / do not) support fining parents of truant students because _____

    _____

    _____

Commonly Misspelled Words

Educated readers are put off by misspelled words. Even a carefully reasoned article or letter lacks credibility if words are misspelled.

It's better to be safe than sorry! All good writers keep a dictionary at hand to quickly resolve any doubts about spelling.

A. Circle the correctly spelled word in each list. Check a dictionary if you're not sure.

1. recieve
   receave
   receive
	4. curiosity
	   curiousity
	   curiossity
		7. phisycal
		   physicle
		   physical

2. goverment
   government
   govurment
	5. exeed
	   excede
	   exceed
		8. label
		   lable
		   labal

3. absence
   absense
   abscense
	6. aquire
	   acquire
	   ackquire
		9. vegatible
		   vegetable
		   vegteble

B. Cross out two misspelled words in each sentence. Rewrite the words correctly on the lines under the sentences.

1. It isn't neccessary to vaccum the carpet every day.

   _____   _____

2. Roger is an excellant interpeter of old Italian manuscripts.

   _____   _____

3. The tempature in the lawndry room must have been 100 degrees!

   _____   _____

4. Stephanie's dormatory is just accross the street from mine.

   _____   _____

5. Rod finds it benifical to write all of his appointments on his desk calender.

_____   _____

6. Eli's roomate this year is a sophmore named Chip Hansen.

_____   _____

7. Paul must take responsability for his childish lack of disipline.

_____   _____

8. To Tiffany, loosing her grandmother's ring was a real tradgedy.

_____   _____

C. Circle the correctly spelled words to complete the sentences.

1. (Mathematics / Mathamatics / Mathmatics) is a core subject in our school's (curriculum / curicculum / curiculam).

2. It's no (suprise / surprise / surprize) that the tellers felt (shakey / shaky / shakie) after the bank robbery.

3. The (rythm / rhythm / rithym) of the Latin dance music was truly (irresistable / irresistible / iresistable).

4. To be (successful / succesful / successfull), you must always (beleive / believe / beleave) in your own ability.

5. I'm sure you can find that (article / artical / artacal) in the main (liberry / library / libarry).

6. The chemistry (labratory / laboratory / laberatory) is (usualy / usually / usally) open from noon to five.

7. Do you know the (definition / defanition / defenition) of the word (*parallel* / *paralell* / *paralel*)?

FINAL PROJECT

Persuasive Essay

WHAT A GREAT OPPORTUNITY!

**Citizens for a Better America is proud to sponsor an essay contest.
The winner will receive a $5,000 SCHOLARSHIP
to a college of his or her choice!**

RULES: 1. Choose a topic that expresses a good idea for improving the lives of Americans.

2. Develop your idea in a minimum of five paragraphs.

3. Write an interesting title for your essay.

4. Warning: Errors in grammar, spelling, and punctuation will be counted against you!

Why not give it a try? — You've got nothing to lose and everything to gain!

---

1. Prewriting: Select a topic.

What subject, or topic, do you have strong personal feelings about? (It's much easier to write persuasively about something that truly interests you!)

Here are some suggestions: Now list some ideas of your own:

•*solar power*   •_____

•*healthy lifestyle*   •_____

•*safe driving*   •_____

•*community service*   •_____

Your final topic choice is: _____

2. Prewriting: Gather details.

Brainstorm before you begin to write. Jot down notes that answer questions such as these:

- Why does the topic seem important to you?
- Can you support your opinions with personal experience?
- Exactly how does it affect the lives of Americans?
- What facts or examples might help you develop your topic?

Check out your topic in books, newspapers, or on the Internet. Take notes on separate note cards, identifying the source of the information. Why? So you can quote your sources accurately in your final essay.

3. Draft your thesis statement.

This is the most important sentence in your introductory paragraph. Its purpose is to interest the reader as it states the topic of the essay. Everything else in the essay works to support your thesis. Usually, the thesis statement will be the last sentence in the introductory paragraph.

Here are two examples of thesis statements:

TOPIC	THESIS STATEMENT
healthy lifestyle	*Americans could live longer, happier lives if they gave up their unhealthy habits.*
community service	*Communities thrive when good neighbors volunteer.*

Your thesis statement is: _____

_____

Once you've written a clear thesis statement, you're on your way! You've stated your point. Now you can begin to prove it with a discussion of your supporting facts and examples. Each reason will be stated in a topic sentence and developed in a paragraph.

4. Draft the body of your essay.

Remember that your essay must have at least five paragraphs. The thesis statement is the topic sentence of your first paragraph. The topic of your final or concluding paragraph should be a restatement of your thesis, using different words. Your conclusion should summarize the material already presented.

Look back through your notes and decide how you want to organize the material you've gathered. (Remember that all your paragraphs must support and expand on the thesis statement!) Then write topic sentences for the middle three paragraphs.

THESIS STATEMENT (PARAGRAPH 1): _____

_____

TOPIC SENTENCE FOR PARAGRAPH 2: _____

_____

TOPIC SENTENCE FOR PARAGRAPH 3: _____

_____

TOPIC SENTENCE FOR PARAGRAPH 4: _____

_____

PARAPHRASE OF YOUR THESIS STATEMENT FOR THE CONCLUSION (PARAGRAPH 5): _____

_____

_____

5. Write an interesting title for your essay.

6. Revise and edit your essay.

Carefully review your work. Look for sentences that need to be rewritten and make notes for revision. Ask yourself questions like these:

- Is my opening strong enough to capture the reader's attention?
- Can I replace poor word choices with words that are more concise or colorful?
- Did I use enough facts and examples to make my opinion convincing?
- Does the style of my writing suit the subject matter?
- Is the body of the essay well-organized?
- Can transitional words and phrases be added to improve the flow of ideas?

7. Ask a peer to review your essay.

Offer to do the same for your classmate. Offering and accepting input can improve *both* of your essays.

8. Proofread your work.

Carefully reread your work for errors in spelling, grammar, and punctuation. Settle for nothing less than perfection in your final draft!

9. Make a final copy and publish it.

Here are some ways you can "publish" your essay before you send it off to the contest judges:

- Read your essay aloud to the class.
- Post a copy on your classroom bulletin board, or on an electronic bulletin board.
- Write an e-mail to your friends, attaching a copy of your essay.

To the Teacher

"Practice is the best of all instructors." —Publilius Syrus, *Maxim*

Let's face it: *Most* students need to improve their writing skills.

All too often, student work is blemished by poorly composed sentences, misspelled words, and punctuation errors. The meaning the student writer intended to convey is unclear, if not downright confusing. What's the solution? The venerable old Roman got it right more than 2,000 years ago: practice, practice, and more practice!

Saddleback's WRITING 4 series links writing to purpose. Each of the four workbooks: NARRATIVE, EXPOSITORY, DESCRIPTIVE, and PERSUASIVE, specifically focuses on one particular "reason for writing." Each workbook contains 21 applications lessons and seven basic skills practice lessons. Relevant applications include drafting personal and business letters, narrating an historical event, and reviewing a movie. Specific skills taught include analyzing your audience, recognizing propaganda, creating tone, and sorting fact and opinion. Fundamental skills and concepts such as main idea, supporting details, and writing introductions and conclusions are reviewed in all four workbooks.

ONGOING ASSESSMENT

Periodic checks of student workbooks are highly recommended. If possible, assign peer tutors to coach remediation.

LESSON EXTENSIONS

To reinforce and enrich the workbook exercises, you may want to assign "extra credit" activities such as the following:

✓ write step-by-step instructions for some task that individual students know how to do, e.g., make a salad, repair a flat tire, etc.

✓ record the stories they write, or read them aloud to students in other classrooms

✓ write independent descriptions of the same event or object; then compare and contrast, discussing viewpoint, vocabulary, and level of detail

✓ bring in "letters to the editor" from newspapers and magazines to analyze and discuss in class

✓ write employment reference letters for each other

✓ critique TV commercials or ads they've seen in the print media

✓ write directions for walking or driving from one point to another, e.g., home to school, library to home, etc.

✓ interview a parent or a school employee, and then "write up" the interview for an article in the school newspaper

ANSWER KEY

LESSON 1: Reasons for Writing (pp. 6–7)

A. 1. Persuasive 2. Narrative 3. Descriptive
 4. Expository

B. Answers will vary.

C. 1. descriptive, mysterious
 2. expository, straightforward
 3. narrative, sarcastic
 4. persuasive, outraged

LESSON 2: Writing to Persuade (pp. 8–9)

A. Circle: • anti-smoking poster

 • army recruitment brochure

 • newspaper editorial

 • movie review

 • political speech

B. Answers will vary.

C. Ranking: _4_ threaten

 _3_ plead

 _2_ entice

 _1_ recommend

 Statement Identification: 1. _T_
 2. _E_
 3. _R_
 4. _P_

D. Answers will vary.

LESSON 3: Propaganda (p. 10–11)

A. 1. T 2. T 3. F 4. F 5. T 6. T

B. Answers will vary.

BASIC SKILLS PRACTICE: Prewriting: Audience Viewpoint (pp. 12–13)

A. 1. acne 2. police officers 3. Security
 4. Adults 5. Minorities 6. Pacifists

B. 1. f 2. d 3. e 4. b 5. c 6. a

C. Answers will vary.

LESSON 4: Writing Persuasive Topic Sentences (pp. 14–15)

A. Answers will vary. Possible answers:

 2. Acneaway is a great new product.

 3. I've learned the hard way that honesty really is the best policy.

 4. Too many commercials can ruin the experience of watching television.

B. Answers will vary. Possible answers:

 1. Vote for Vic Vargas, an honest man!

 2. The museum is a wonderful place to visit.

 3. It takes more skill and talent to ski than to ice skate.

 4. Every consumer needs to know the facts about credit card debt.

 5. *The Revenge of the Earthworms* premiered last night.

C. Answers will vary. Possible answers:

 1. Mike Mack is a better quarterback than Wally White.

 2. Instant weight loss products are usually a sham.

 3. Apologize to Dad right away.

LESSON 5: Persuasive Paragraphs 1 (pp. 16–17)

A. 1. c, d 2. b, d 3. b, d

B. Answers will vary. Possible answers:

 POSSIBLE TOPIC SENTENCE:
 Babe Ruth was one of baseball's all-time greats.

 POSSIBLE BODY OF THE PARAGRAPH:
 Babe Ruth will always be remembered as one of baseball's greatest players. During the 1927 season alone, he hit 60 home runs. In his 21-year career, he hit 714 home runs and batted in 2,209 runs. He played in 10 World Series and held 76 all-time major league records.

C. and D. Answers will vary.

LESSON 6: Persuasive Paragraphs 2 (pp. 18–19)

A. Sentences that do *not* support topic sentence:

 • The free public library in our town is located at the corner of Fifth and Oak.

 • A fee of 25 cents is charged for each day a borrowed book is overdue.

B. Possible replacement sentences follow sentence to be cross out:

1. SENTENCE TO BE CROSSED OUT:
   Attractive nylon sweatsuits are very popular at health clubs and gyms.
   POSSIBLE REPLACEMENT SENTENCE:
   Aerobic activities such as swimming, dancing, and many sports can increase your metabolism and help in weight loss.

2. SENTENCE TO BE CROSSED OUT:
   Michael's twin sisters, Rose and Gale, will attend our school next year.
   POSSIBLE REPLACEMENT SENTENCE:
   His previous leadership experience in various clubs has prepared him for this position.

C. Answers will vary. Possible answers:

1. Instead of pouring funds into the bottomless pit of space exploration, we should work on improving human lives here on planet Earth.

2. It is imperative that we work to free all Americans from the damaging effects of tobacco addiction.

D. Answers will vary.

BASIC SKILLS PRACTICE: Redundancy (pp. 20–21)

A. Answers will vary. Possible answers:

1. School starts at 8:00 A.M. and ends at 3:00 P.M.

2. Rafael is a preschool student.

3. Trees can be pruned during any season.

4. The broken chain on Henry's bike must be replaced.

5. Do you ever reminisce about your childhood?

6. A German girl lives next door to me.

B. Answers will vary. Possible answers:

1. The fastest swimmer will proudly accept the award.

2. Carefully consider each answer before you decide.

3. All athletes must follow Coach Gordon's rules.

4. Harold wants to add potato salad to the picnic lunch.

5. Emily's classmates elected her class president.

6. They agreed to go out for pizza after the game.

7. Yesterday's homework assignment is due on Monday.

LESSON 7: Facts and Opinions (pp. 22–23)

A. Answers will vary. Check work to make sure student has written a statement of *fact* or *opinion* as directed.

B. Answers will vary. Check work to make sure student has written a statement of *opinion*—<u>not</u> one of fact.

C. Answers will vary. Possible answers:

1. *It is likely* that flooding will occur if the rain doesn't stop soon.

2. *Many* citizens *appear* to be unhappy with the governor's performance.

3. *In my opinion*, the death penalty is unjust and inhumane.

4. Victoria was *probably* the greatest queen in English history.

5. *I think* lilacs have a sweeter scent than roses.

6. *Apparently* migraine headaches are caused by stress.

7. *Supposedly* that face cream makes wrinkles disappear overnight.

8. *It seems* that *some* voters are suspicious of that candidate's record.

LESSON 8: Letters to the Editor (pp. 24–25)

A. 1. F 2. T 3. T 4. F 5. T 6. T 7. F 8. F 9. T 10. T

B. Answers will vary. Possible answers:

1. No, because the writer is clearly deranged.

2. No, because the reader's objection is foolish.

3. Yes, because the reader's suggestion is sensible and timely.

C. Answers will vary.

LESSON 9: Movie Review (pp. 26–27)

Answers will vary. Check work to make sure student has accomplished the threefold job of a good movie review: to inform, to evaluate, and to recommend.

BASIC SKILLS PRACTICE: Frequently Confused Words (pp. 28–29)

A. Answers will vary. Make sure required words are used correctly.

B. 1. all together
2. altogether
3. Everyone
4. every one
5. all ready
6. already
7. sometime
8. some time

C. 1. social
2. implied
3. farther
4. take

LESSON 10: Working World 1 (pp. 30–31)

A. Answers will vary. Make sure student's work includes the four required elements of a good letter of application.

B. 1. friendly, businesslike
2. long, messy
3. plain white
4. effort

C. Answers will vary. Possible answer:

Dear Ms. Gomez:

It was a pleasure to meet you. I appreciate your time and certainly hope I get an interview for the counselor's job.

I've always enjoyed working with kids, and I know quite a bit about sports and crafts. If you hire me, I will do a great job. Did I tell you that my career goal is to become a teacher?

I look forward to your call.

Sincerely,

LESSON 11: Working World 2 (pp. 32–33)

A. Circle: reliable, hardworking, cooperative, determined, energetic, honest

B. Answers will vary. Make sure student has made a serious attempt to create a fair yet impressive reference letter for the "former employee."

C. and D. Answers will vary. Make sure student has listed thoughtful and realistic skills, accomplishments, and personal qualities, and written a letter of recommendation that reflects an equal level of sincerity and honesty.

LESSON 12: Working World 3 (pp. 34–35)

A. and B. Answers will vary. Make sure student has included appropriate support for the purpose of each memo.

C. Examples of statements that should *not* be in a memo requesting a raise:

1. I need more money for the lifestyle I want.
2. My roommate is driving me crazy. I want to get a place of my own.
3. My car broke down. If you want me to be here on time, you'll have to give me more money.

BASIC SKILLS PRACTICE: Capitalization (pp. 36–37)

A. 1. During World War II, many citizens of Europe went hungry.
2. Have you tried the new Greek restaurant on Tenth Avenue?
3. Martin said, "This school doesn't offer many history courses."
4. The Internal Revenue Service collects federal taxes.
5. The headquarters of the American Cancer Society has been relocated.
6. Paul studies government at Marshall High School in Chicago.
7. His brother and sister live with their dad on Grand Boulevard.

B. 1. My uncle was a sergeant in the U.S. Army.
2. Gone with the Wind will be screened at 2:10 P.M.
3. Dr. Joseph McKenna, D.D.S., opened his office in May.
4. Sir Lawrence Olivier was a brilliant English actor.
5. No one recognized Aunt Polly in her clever Halloween costume.
6. Grace M. Johnson, a professor, earned her Ph.D. at Indiana University.
7. I read "The Charge of the Light Brigade" in my British Literature class.

LESSON 13: Advertising 1 (pp. 38–39)

A. and B. Answers will vary.

C. Answers will vary. Possible answers:

1. ~~Pretentious~~ *Elite* cars for ~~pretentious~~ *elite* people
2. ~~Cramped~~ *Cozy* seaside cottage . . .
3. ~~Brittle, fatty-flavored~~ *Crisp, buttery* fried chicken
4. The ~~glare~~ *glow* . . . absolutely ~~blinding~~ *brilliant.*
5. ~~Cheap~~ *Thrifty* shoppers . . .

D. Answers will vary. Possible answers:

1. Spring Morning perfume ~~reeks~~ *smells* . . .
2. GoodGargle . . . ~~scrubs~~ *cleans* your breath.
3. ~~Hoard~~ *Save* your money . . .

LESSON 14: Advertising 2 (pp. 40–41)

Answers will vary.

LESSON 15: Letter of Complaint (pp. 42–43)

A. and C. Answers will vary.

B. POSSIBLE ANSWERS:

2. If I don't receive a refund within two weeks, I will report your store to the Better Business Bureau.
3. Both the materials and workmanship in your Mighty Muscle Treadmill are of poor quality.

BASIC SKILLS PRACTICE: Connotation and Denotation (pp. 44–45)

A. 1. plainspoken   3. shy

    2. delicate   4. enthusiastic

B. 1. d   2. f   3. e   4. c   5. a   6. b

C.

POSITIVE	NEGATIVE
2. classic	outdated
3. revolutionary	unproven
4. playful	silly
5. assertive	aggressive
6. wary	suspicious
7. persistent	stubborn
8. daring	reckless

LESSON 16: Public Service Appeal (pp. 46–47)

A. Answers will vary.

B. Answers will vary. Possible answers:

2. Just give us a call and our driver will pick up the clothes from your doorstep.
3. If you can read, you can help. We welcome all reading tutors, whether you're 16 or 60!
4. All we're asking is a commitment of two hours a week.

LESSON 17: Personal Letters 1 (pp. 48–49)

A. Letter content will vary. Check to make sure student has used proper writing guidelines. The following spelling errors should all have been corrected:

Mrs. Henderson,

    I'm the guy who smashed your window yesterday. My mom says you're ~~realy~~ really steamed at me. That's why she's ~~makeing~~ making me ~~right~~ write this letter.

    I told her the ball I hit ~~threw~~ through your window was a home run! But did she ~~congradgulate~~ congratulate me? No ~~weigh~~ way! It's just a ~~peace~~ piece of glass. A ~~knew~~ new window ~~pain~~ pane won't cost you much. And hey—it was an ~~aksident~~ accident! Give me a ~~brake~~ break!

       Your ~~niehbor~~ neighbor,

       Lefty Louis

P.S. When can I get my ball back?

B. Letter content will vary. Check to make sure student has used proper writing guidelines and that there are no grammar, punctuation, or spelling errors.

LESSON 18: Personal Letters 2 (pp. 50–51)

B. Content of letters will vary. Check to make sure student has used proper writing guidelines and that there are no grammar, punctuation, or spelling errors.

Basic Skills Practice: Verbs: Agreement with Subject (pp. 52–53)

A. 1. competes 2. is 3. are 4. was
5. differ 6. is

B. Student sentences will vary. Make sure verb agrees with indefinite pronoun.

1. apply, are 2. is 3. take 4. have
5. are 6. has 7. is

Lesson 19: Debate 1: Pros and Cons (pp. 54–55)

A. 1. contrast 2. fact 3. example
4. analogy 5. comparison

B. and C. Answers will vary.

Lesson 20: Debate 2: Developing an Argument (pp. 56–57)

Answers will vary. Check work to make sure student has properly supported his or her argument by using reasonable facts, examples, contrasts, comparisons, or analogies.

Lesson 21: Candidate's Speech (pp. 58–59)

Answers will vary. Check work to make sure student has properly supported his or her position by using reasonable facts, examples, contrasts, comparisons, or analogies.

Basic Skills Practice: Commonly Misspelled Words (pp. 60–61)

A. 1. receive   6. acquire

2. government   7. physical

3. absence   8. label

4. curiosity   9. vegetable

5. exceed

B. 1. necessary, vacuum

2. excellent, interpreter

3. temperature, laundry

4. dormitory, across

5. beneficial, calendar

6. roommate, sophomore

7. responsibility, discipline

8. losing, tragedy

C. 1. Mathematics, curriculum

2. surprise, shaky

3. rhythm, irresistible

4. successful, believe

5. article, library

6. laboratory, usually

7. definition, parallel

Final Project: Persuasive Essay (pp. 62–64)

Answers will vary.